Games and Activities for Exploring Feelings with Children

Games and Activities for Exploring Feelings with Children

Giving Children the Confidence to
Navigate Emotions and Friendships

Vanessa Rogers

Jessica Kingsley *Publishers*
London and Philadelphia

First published in 2011
by Jessica Kingsley Publishers
116 Pentonville Road
London N1 9JB, UK
and
400 Market Street, Suite 400
Philadelphia, PA 19106, USA

www.jkp.com

Library of Congress Cataloging in Publication Data
Rogers, Vanessa.
  Games and activities for exploring feelings with children : giving children the confidence
to navigate emotions and friendships / Vanessa Rogers.
      p. cm.
  ISBN 978-1-84905-222-1 (alk. paper)
  1. Emotions in children. 2. Social interaction in children. 3. Child psychology. I. Title.
  BF723.E6.R64 2011
  372.82--dc22
                          2010054255

British Library Cataloguing in Publication Data
A CIP catalogue record for this book is available from the British Library

ISBN 978 1 84905 222 1

Printed and bound in Great Britain

Contents

Acknowledgements

With many thanks to Zoey Caldwell, Ann McKay, Ingrid Davies, Nicky Hardwick, Ben Carr and Lorraine Clark (Young Citizens Project, North), Charlotte Rogers, Jeanette Williams (Young Citizens Project, South), Anie Twigg (Hertfordshire Careers Service Ltd), Deborah Morgan and Kevin Stewart (Hertfordshire County Council (HCC) Youth Offending Team, North Herts), Gillian Porter (QE11), Tony Hunt (HCC Learning Services), Sophie and Toby Oakes-Rogers (Mill Mead School), Martin Cooke and Mary Westgate (HCC Youth Service), and Deborah Mulroney (HCC Education Department).

And any youth workers not mentioned who have been part of the projects that are referred to.

About the Author

Vanessa is a qualified teacher and youth worker with a Master's degree in community education. She has over ten years' experience within the Hertfordshire Youth Service both at practitioner and management levels. Prior to achieving national recognition for her work, Vanessa managed a wide range of services for young people including a large youth centre and targeted detached projects for Hertfordshire County Council. She devises and delivers professional development training programmes and writes for *Youth Work Now*. In addition, she has been commissioned to devise training packs for a wide range of organisations, including the BBC.

This book is one of 20 resources written by Vanessa to support the development of creative youth work and social education.

Her website, www.vanessarogers.co.uk, gives detailed information about further titles, training and consultancy visits.

Introduction

This diverse collection of ideas has been put together to encourage children and young teenagers to talk about their feelings, build self-esteem and develop emotional well-being. It is packed with games and activities that help children to make sense of their experiences, both at home and in the community, and to express themselves positively.

The book aims to help professionals engage with children and young people aged 7–13 years who may not take up statutory services, such as social care or child and adolescent mental health services, but who could respond well to an informal education youth work approach – an approach that draws on the tradition of exploring social and political issues while having fun.

Many of the issues identified for this younger target group are familiar themes: young people hanging around on street corners, anti-social behaviour, difficulties experienced with peer relationships and bullying, educational under-achievement and low self-esteem. The major difference is that these are increasingly seen as issues of concern with children of a younger age, rather than during the more turbulent teenage years. This is especially important if we are to ensure that young people are diverted away from offending behaviour and reduce the numbers entering the criminal justice system as much as possible.

Early intervention and a trusted adult to talk to are key to effective preventative work, and this resource is ideal for all those working with vulnerable children, including social workers, teachers, youth workers and counsellors.

Most activities can be used for individual or group work, and are easily adapted as appropriate.

Making the rules

These 'rules' set the scene for any programme of work and encourage children to explore their expectations and consider ways to make sessions as successful as possible. They also offer facilitators the opportunity to set boundaries and explain professional confidentiality.

Also included in this section are suggestions for developing action plans with children, helping both the worker and the young person assess need, set goals and celebrate success.

Getting to know each other

The worksheets and activities contained in this section enable children and young people to start considering the people and things that are important to them. These can be positive and negative experiences and you need to be sure that the young person is clear about the boundaries of your confidentiality and at what stage you will need to pass on information.

These sessions also offer the opportunity for workers to stress that working together is on a voluntary basis and not a punishment because people think they are 'bad children' or have been 'naughty'. It is a good time to reassure the young people about your role and encourage them to identify positive outcomes for themselves. Building a positive relationship now is important to the success of future work.

Expressing yourself

This section focuses on supporting young people in recognising and expressing their feelings. This includes ways to recognise how others are feeling, encouraging empathy and understanding.

The baseline for all the sessions is the recognition that everyone has a wide range of feelings and emotions that are responses to both internal and external factors. These include emotions such as love and happiness as well as fear and anger, and each session underlines the right to feel these. Some sessions focus on specific feelings and seek to explore personal 'triggers', before considering positive ways to cope.

The activities encourage young people to look at different ways of expressing themselves and to reflect on what motivates them.

Making friends

Peer relationships and friendships are very important to young people. This chapter contains activities and worksheets that explore the impact and value of these. Working together and 'positive play' are strands that run through all the games and team building activities. These encourage young people to share resources with others, support friends through a task and realise what can be achieved by working together.

The sessions support children in considering the things that contribute to both positive and negative relationships and how they can effect change. This includes peer pressure and encourages the ability to say 'no', thereby helping children to recognise qualities required for friendship and to consider trust, honesty and reciprocity.

Personal responsibility, loyalty and honesty are all discussed, encouraging children to think through the likely consequences of their actions and the impact actions can have on others.

Endings

The activities suggested in this final section aim to close group or individual sessions on a positive note. They offer feedback for workers to consider the success of the programme, and give the children a chance to reflect on what they have just participated in.

Chapter 1

Making the Rules

Parent/guardian consent

It is good practice to obtain a consent form for work with all young people, but if you are starting a piece of work with a child under 13 it is vital. Consent needs to be given by whoever has parental responsibility for the young person. This can be a parent, but could be another relative such as a grandparent, foster carer or a named social worker. Whoever it is, make sure that the person has signed the form and given you as much information about the child as possible before you start.

The consent form should clearly state who you are, what the aims of the sessions are and where they will be held. It is also important to find out about any medication that may be needed during the young person's time with you. As well as medication needed during the session, such as an inhaler for asthma, it is also useful to know if a child has regular treatment for a condition, such as Ritalin for attention deficit hyperactivity disorder (ADHD). All of this will inform the sessions that you plan.

Try to find out about likely responses to difficult or emotional situations. Obviously you are not planning to deliberately upset the child, but emotions can run high and it is good to know who copes well in a group, who prefers personal space and any history of aggressive outbursts or other behaviour that may require an additional risk assessment.

Finally, make sure that you have a contact number you can reach while the sessions are on in the event of an emergency. Then, if there is an accident or a problem later, you have the information to hand with which to support the young people.

Explaining the need

Lots of people are put off contact with agencies if they think that it involves lots of paperwork or form filling. It is important to explain to young people and their families why you are asking for consent.

If you are planning home visits to meet the young people and their families before starting any work, you could take the consent forms with you. This offers the opportunity to explain fully what it is you are going to be doing and encourages both the children and parents or carers to ask any questions they may have.

You can also make sure that any expectations are realistic on both sides. For example, if young people have been refusing to go to school for several months, it is unlikely they will go the next day just because you have visited!

By having these discussions now, parents, carers and young people can make informed choices as to whether they want to take part or not.

During the session

One worker should assume responsibility for keeping the consent forms for the duration of the session. If you plan to facilitate a block of sessions, put all the dates and details on the consent forms so that they only have to go home once for signing.

Consent forms should be kept in a confidential file along with any other paperwork relating to the young people, including risk assessments and any evaluation sheets used by your organisation to review progress.

CONSENT FORM

Worker's name . . . .

Telephone number . . . . Date . . . .

The aim of meeting is to . . . .

. . . .

. . . .

Dates . . . . Time . . . .

Venue . . . .

I give consent for . . . .

(full name of young person) to be allowed to take part in this project and to participate in the activities involved.

I understand these will include sessions on:

- developing interpersonal skills
- team building and group work
- anti-social behaviour and consequences of actions
- building self-confidence and raising self-esteem
- managing anger and expressing feelings
- peer pressure and bullying developing interpersonal skills.

Medical conditions

Has . . . . (first name of young person) any medical conditions that may need treatment during a session? Yes/No

If 'yes', please give details . . . .

. . . .

Has . . . . (first name) any known allergies? Yes/No

If 'yes', please give details . . . .

. . . .

Date of last immunisation against tetanus . . . .

National Health Service (NHS) Medical Card Number

. . . .

Is there any other information that you think we should have (e.g. behaviour, fears, likes or dislikes)? Yes/No

If 'yes', please give details . . . .

. . . .

If necessary, do you give consent for emergency medical treatment? Yes/No

Signature . . . . (parent or guardian)

Date . . . .

Address . . . .

. . . .

Telephone numbers (home) . . . .

(mobile) . . . .

If you have any queries or would like to discuss anything further, please contact me on . . . .

Anti-oppressive practice

To ensure that you can meet the needs of the young people you are planning to work with, it is a good idea to consider what barriers there may be to their accessing your provision.

For some young people you will need to consider their cultural or religious backgrounds and decide if the work you are hoping to do will meet their needs. For example, will the family be comfortable with where you are planning to meet? Does this need to be a single gender group? Would the young person be happier working with someone of the same religion or culture? If you think there may be issues, consult the young people and their families in advance to discuss and agree options.

Consider gender issues and, if appropriate, offer the option of a same-sex worker. This can be especially important if a child has a history of bad relationships with a particular gender, or is known to social services as a child protection case.

Make sure that the building and space you plan to work in are appropriate for the young person. Most new buildings have good access for wheelchair users, but older buildings can be more difficult to get into. Similarly, facilities, such as toilets, need to be suitable.

As well as physical disabilities, consider children you may be working with who have conduct disorders or who are liable to 'run' at some point during the work. Good pointers to the suitability of a building are things like:

1. Is the area clear so that the children can run and play without tripping or damaging anything?

2. Is the building excessively hot or does it have poor lighting? Both of these can add to the likelihood of challenging behaviour.

3. Does the building face straight onto a main road? What precautions can you take to prevent an accident?

4. Have you agreed an action plan with the parents or carers and your co-worker in the event of a young person running off?

All these issues can be discussed beforehand and agreements copied and sent to everyone. Additionally, you may want to do a risk assessment for particular activities.

Working together

Before you start, discuss expectations of the children and boundaries and strategies for managing challenging behaviour with your co-worker. This is an extremely important part of the planning process because it allows time for discussions around behavioural expectations and any sanctions, resulting in a co-ordinated staff team with shared values. This in turn will give a clear message to the children that will help them to feel safe and to build positive, respectful relationships.

Group rules

It is a good idea to start work with any group by agreeing some ground rules or a contract that everyone signs up to. Group rules are not the same as the non-negotiable rules or regulations that are either statutory or set by management committees. These tend to be around health and safety or legal requirements, such as child protection procedures. Make sure that both workers and young people are aware of the difference and know the boundaries to your confidentiality.

Good group rules consist of ways that young people and workers can work together to enjoy sessions and create a safe and supportive environment. Group rules set boundaries so that everyone can learn effectively together, but they also provide opportunities for the whole group to participate in something that has a clear outcome.

It can be a difficult process to engage young people who have only just come together, but a contract needs to be facilitated at an early stage in the life of the group. Spending time looking at the things that really matter to the young people is a worthwhile task, even if it does seem extremely hard work at times! With younger children you may need to be more creative to get a good response.

Workers should participate in the process but not hijack it with their own rules. The point is to create a framework that everyone is happy with and feels comfortable working within.

Children should be supported in considering the following:

- Everyone joins the group bringing different life experiences and values.

- It is important to listen to each other and respect each other's opinions and ideas.

- If the group is to be effective everyone needs the opportunity to take part.

- The group is a safe place to experiment with new ideas and activities and to make a mistake is okay.

- What happens within the group stays within it, apart from child protection issues.

If new members join the group, you will need to review the group rules to make sure that any needs or ideas that they have are considered. Similarly, new workers will need to agree to the contract.

1.1 Group graffiti wall

This is good fun, but you will need to assess the children's or young people's literacy skills to make sure they are not going to feel daunted by the task.

Aim

To produce a set of group rules to which everyone has contributed.

You will need

- a large wall
- flipchart sheets
- marker pens.

How to do it

Cover two separate areas of wall with flipchart paper and lay out a good selection of marker pens before the young people arrive. Divide the group into two and explain the task and importance of developing a group contract. If you think that the children may need some prompts, write some questions to stimulate thoughts on the graffiti sheets in advance. For example:

- What would make this group good for you?
- How do you like people to talk to you?
- What will you do to make this group a success?

Once everyone is clear what is required, hand out pens – and stand well back!

Explain that no one has the right to alter or erase someone else's comments – there will be space to challenge and reach agreement at the end. Suggest that points already made can be agreed with by putting a tick, and ensure that everybody participates and nobody takes over the wall.

Once the space has been filled, ask the group members to stand back and review what they have produced. Are there common themes? How many ticks are there? Does anyone want to talk about what they have written or ask about anything on the wall?

Pull out the main themes from both sheets and agree a set of group rules that incorporates everybody's ideas. This can be written up onto another sheet.

Finally, take up the pens again and ask each member of the group (including staff) to sign and date the contract. Display during group time as a reminder of agreements made.

1.2 Individual contracts

Contracts tend to be associated with group work, but it is also a good place to start when you are planning to work individually with a child or young person. The process allows space for the young people to question why they are with you and to express what they would like to achieve.

Aim

The point of this session is to gain an understanding from young people of what they see as their issues and what they hope to gain from contact with you.

You will need

- a copy of the 'contract circle'

- pens.

How to do it

Introduce the idea that, to make the sessions really useful to the young people, you need to identify areas that they would like to work on together. Encourage them to take ownership of their contracts so that they become useful pieces of work, not things imposed upon them.

Suggest that the 'contract' is a two-way process that looks at what you will do to make the sessions productive, and identifies each young person's responsibilities in the process. Hand out a copy of the 'contract circle'.

Use the headings to prompt discussion and support the young people in identifying achievable goals. Use the contracts to review progress in later meetings.

CONTRACT CIRCLE

How I like to learn

Things I agree to do

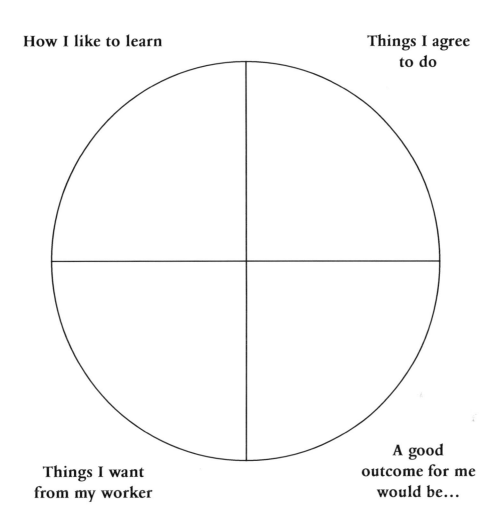

Things I want from my worker

A good outcome for me would be...

1.3 My action plan

Action plans enable children and young people to focus on areas that they would like to work on. These can be personal goals, such as learning a new skill, or part of a specific programme – for example, looking at anger management or offending behaviour.

Aim

This activity engages children in setting goals and involves them in the decision-making process about how they spend their time with you.

You will need

- pens
- a copy of the the 'my action plan' sheet.

How to do it

Make sure that you set aside time when you can work through the action plan process with each young person quietly.

Explain that the point of this session is to devise action plans that belong to the young people. Reassure them that the plans are lists of things that other people think are 'wrong', but that they offer a chance to spend time concentrating on goals that are important to them personally. It is also the opportunity to explain the boundaries to your confidentiality and when information will be shared.

Hand out a copy of the 'my action plan' sheet and a selection of pens to each child. Encourage them all to personalise the sheets in any way they want – for example, decorating the blank spaces, or drawing pictures of things important to them.

Now, support the young people in completing the sheets. Encourage them to set themselves specific, realistic goals so that they do not become disappointed or disinterested in the first week. For example, rather than writing, 'I will never get into trouble at school again', it might be more achievable to say, 'I will use the "time out" system in class, rather than walking out of school.'

Stress that the action plan is not about 'failing', but about personal goals and achievements. Make sure that the young people can see the personal benefits from any goal reached by considering 'celebrations' of targets met.

Finally, an action plan is intended as a working document, so it can be revised or updated at any time. Build in review dates so that you can see if goals are being achieved and when a new action plan is needed.

MY ACTION PLAN

This is your action plan to look at the things that are important to you. Choose things that *you* would like to work on. Be realistic and focus on things that you think you can do and remember to celebrate your successes!

What do I hope to achieve? . . . .
. . . .
. . . .

How could I do it? . . . .
. . . .
. . . .

What support would I like? . . . .
. . . .
. . . .

How long will it take? . . . .
. . . .
. . . .

How will I know if I have been successful? . . . .

. . . .

. . . .

What could stop me? . . . .

. . . .

. . . .

How will I celebrate my achievements? . . . .

. . . .

. . . .

My name . . . . Date . . . .

Chapter 2

Getting to Know Each Other

2.1 Introduction circle

This form of introduction works well with all ages, but for the best effect you need a group of at least six and plenty of space to sit down.

Aim

This is a warm-up intended to introduce group members to each other and the facilitators. You may want to make a ground rule that everyone must be included in the exercise before you start so that no one gets left out.

You will need

- a ball of brightly coloured wool.

How to do it

Make a large circle, placing the adult leaders at a distance within the group. Keeping a tight hold of the loose end, throw the ball of wool randomly to another member of the group. As you do so, welcome the person and introduce yourself. For example, 'Welcome to the group, my name is Krishna'. The second person should return the greeting in a similar way – for example, 'Welcome Krishna, my name is Jamie' – before throwing the ball of wool to the next member and repeating the process. Make sure that each person keeps a hold on the wool before throwing the main ball on. Continue until each person has been welcomed and introduced.

As the exercise progresses, you will begin to see a web forming that traces the path of the wool.

Finally, ask the young people to put the web down on the ground and step away. Ask them to look at and reflect on the 'social' web that they have made. To extend the activity, invite them to re-wind the ball of wool by re-tracing its path and re-introducing each group member.

2.2 My timeline

The idea of this one-to-one exercise is to enable children to 'map' the important things that have happened to them so far, and so explore major events in their lives.

Aim

This process enables children and young people to discuss, in a safe environment, things that have happened to them. They ultimately choose how much they want to share.

You will need

- flipchart paper taped together to make timelines for the wall

- marker pens.

How to do it

Before the young people arrive, prepare the 'timelines' by taping flipchart sheets together end-to-end along a large stretch of wall. Make sure these are set at a height that can be reached comfortably. With a thick black marker, halfway down each timeline, write the words 'BIRTH' at the start of the timeline and 'NOW' at the end. Draw a straight line between the two points.

Explain what the aim of a timeline is and what you are trying to produce together. Indicate the straight black line between the two points. Ask the young people to consider if their lives have been 'straight lines' – that is, nothing happening and feelings and events staying the same – or if there have been a series of high and low points that move either side of their lines. Conclude that this is normal and that most people have good and not so good experiences.

Invite the young people to write important landmarks on their timelines to reflect how they feel about them, with positive things above and less positive below. This should include anything that has had an impact – for example, starting school, the birth of a brother or sister, parents divorcing or the death of a pet. Encourage the children to include religious celebrations and important events within their culture.

Once the timelines are complete, encourage the young people to stand back and look at what has been produced. Discuss the highs and lows and how they have an impact on the present, including how issues could be resolved.

2.3 My desert island

This method of 'mapping' can be used with young people of any age or gender and it works just as well in a group or individually. Because it uses pictures, it is ideal for engaging with those who find writing difficult.

Aim

This exercise helps to identify the important people in the life of a young person.

You will need

- flipchart paper
- marker pens
- stickers, glitter, string, etc. (optional).

How to do it

Explain to the group members that you are giving them a once in a lifetime opportunity to create their own personal desert island! Go on to say that they can take anyone they like to the island, including friends, family and even pets! At this stage do say that you will be inviting everyone to share island pictures later, if this is appropriate.

Hand out the paper and art equipment. Make sure you point out that this not a drawing class and it does not matter if people use pictures, words or a mixture of both.

Allow about 15 minutes for all the children to draw their islands and start to place people where they want them. Ask questions, but remember that all families are different; show sensitivity to whom is represented on the island and how the young people approach the task. Next, ask them to draw themselves next to the people they would like to be closest to on the island.

Finally, give permission for the children to put anyone they don't want on their islands into the sea! You can expand upon this by introducing sharks into the water or boats to allow those they like to see occasionally to visit their islands.

Once the group has finished, ask everyone if they would like to share their islands with the other young people. If there is reluctance to share in a large group you could do this part in pairs. Are there similar choices for whom is chosen? Who stays and who is in the sea? Whom do they want to be with?

2.4 Spider's web map

This is a version of the 'My desert island' that we developed for use with young people aged ten years and older, who may be reluctant to create islands. It uses the same idea – the closer the people in the web are to the 'spider' the more the children like and trust them. Those at the outskirts of the web are people whom they are less happy with.

Aim

To produce a 'map' that shows young people's families and friends and the relationships they have with them.

You will need

- a large sheet of paper
- coloured felt pens.

How to do it

Explain to the young people the purpose of the 'Spider's web map' activity. Suggest that for this exercise they are the 'spider' before asking them to choose a coloured pen and draw a spider in the middle of the paper. Stress that this is not a drawing class, so it does not matter how the spider is drawn – it could just be a coloured dot!

Now, using a different colour, ask the children to draw lines of 'web' to the people who are important to them. Explain that people whom they are close to – for example a parent or best friend – should be shown close to the 'spider'. People whom they are not so keen on can be shown at the end of longer web lines.

Allow about ten minutes, dependent on the ages of the children, to think through the process and map everyone. Once they have all finished, use the map as a starting point for discussion, particularly looking at the choices they have made.

2.5 Share/not share

This session can be used as either a group or individual activity. It is easily adapted to make the game age-appropriate for younger children by changing the topics for discussion.

Aim

The aim of the exercise is to promote discussion about what personal information is appropriate to share, and how this can differ depending on individual 'comfort zones' and relationships.

You will need

- three pieces of card headed 'Share with family', 'Share with friends' and 'Keep to self'

- a set of 'Share/not share' notes made by writing the list suggested onto individual Post-its®.

How to do it

Explain to the young people that this is basically a 'sorting' game. There are no wrong or right answers because it is up to individuals how much personal information they choose to share. Suggest that information is shared at different points in a relationship – for example, choosing to share things with a close friend but not with a new member of class.

Place the three headed cards in front of the group in a line from left to right and distribute the 'Share/not share' Post-it notes.

Invite the children in turn to place each Post-it note under the headed card that they think reflects their thoughts best, inviting reasons and discussion as you go along. Make the proviso that if any children are unsure as to which heading a note should go under, they can 'pass' and return to the note when they have had time to think about or discuss it. You can facilitate this process by questioning or challenging decisions and asking the children to explain their decisions.

The game ends when all the notes are sorted. Conclude by suggesting that it is a good idea to filter information shared so that important things are only told to trusted people.

Suggestions for 'Share/not share' notes

1. I hate meeting new people.

2. I am worried that my body is changing.

3. I am scared to go to school.

4. I am frightened of the dark.

5. I think I am ugly.

6. I wish I was taller.

7. I wish I was thinner.

8. I am worried about how much alcohol my mum drinks.

9. I don't know how my body works.

10. I can't read very well.

11. I have been caught stealing from shops.

12. I have been selected for the school team.

13. I often pretend that I've eaten when I haven't.

14. I want to do well at school.

15. I have head lice.

16. I don't want to live at home anymore.

17. I told my sister a lie.

18. I borrowed something and lost it.

19. I am not sure what a French kiss is.

20. I have inherited £5000.

21. I often feel that I can't cope.

22. I find it hard to make friends.

23. My friends all know more about sex than me.

24. I find it hard to sleep at night.

25. I am on report at school.

2.6 Secrets

This activity is most effective during individual work with a young person whom you know well. Be sensitive to what may arise from the session – you are asking children to share their thoughts with you. Ensure that the young people are clear about your boundaries around confidentiality and that you are clear about what procedures and guidelines you need to follow should they disclose.

Aim

The aim of this activity is to encourage young people to consider the difference between 'good' and 'bad' secrets.

You will need

- two pieces of paper marked 'Good secret' and 'Bad secret'
- Post-it notes with 'secrets' on
- pens
- spare Post-it notes.

How to do it

Introduce the session to children by talking about secrets. Make sure that you are clear what their understanding of a secret is. Then, introduce the idea of different kinds of secrets. Are they aware of any differences?

Now explain that you are going to play a 'sorting game'. Show the young people the Post-it notes and point out that there is a different 'secret' on each. Some are gender-specific so you will need to change them as appropriate. Hand the notes over and ask the children to stick the secrets into two piles, 'Good secrets' and 'Bad secrets'. If they are unsure of where one should go, invite them to stick it somewhere in the middle.

Keep a dialogue going throughout the process, asking the children to explain their decisions and talking through any issues raised. Once they have completed the task, review with them what has happened.

Consider inviting the children to devise their own examples and stick these in the appropriate areas to check learning and understanding. Conclude that some things should not be kept a secret, and emphasise the importance of finding a trusted adult to tell. Record any concerns or issues that need to be raised at the next session.

Suggestions for 'secrets'

Your brother smashed a window at home and has told you not to tell anyone.	You have disobeyed your parents by going somewhere you are not allowed.	It is your mate's birthday and her mum is going to throw a surprise party.
You have caught your sister smoking – she begs you not to tell your dad.	You have hidden all your family's Christmas presents under your bed.	Your friend went shoplifting and gave you loads of stuff to hide.
Your friend has stolen money from school – she says she will go halves with you if you don't tell.	At youth club someone breaks into the tuck shop and steals the sweets. You are offered cheap chocolate at school.	At school the whole class is kept in because of something you did. Everyone blames another classmate and puts pressure on them to own up.

You haven't done your homework so you tell your teacher you have lost your book.	A boy phones but you don't want to speak so you get your sister to say you are out.	The phone bill arrives and it is really high – you tell everyone that it was not you.
You tell your mum you came top in a maths test – you didn't.	Your mum locks you in your room if you behave badly.	You really like a TV show that all your friends hate.
Your friend said she was playing at your house – but she went down the town.	You are spending your dinner money on chocolate and crisps.	Someone is trying to make you do something you don't want to.
You have a secret diary that you write all your thoughts in.	You arrive home late and lie about where you have been.	You and your sister plan a treat for your mum for Mother's Day.
School sent home a letter marked 'Urgent – for attention of Parent only' but you opened it.	You accidentally damaged something you borrowed and gave it back without owning up.	You see your dad kiss another woman at Christmas – he insists you don't tell anyone.
You want to send a Valentine card to someone at school.	Your sister tells you she may be pregnant.	You have a major crush on someone at school.

2.7 The truth, the whole truth...

This worksheet explores the sensitive issue of telling the truth and honesty. It works best in one-to-one settings because children can be more open about their feelings without any peer pressure.

Aim

This activity provokes discussion about the possible consequences of telling the truth or choosing to lie.

You will need

- a copy of 'the truth, the whole truth...' worksheet
- pens.

How to do it

Start the session with a brief discussion about the difference between telling the truth and lying. Make sure that you are clear about the child's understanding and be prepared to explore issues raised – for example, adults not telling the truth to the child in the past.

Hand out a copy of the worksheet and a pen. Consider the young person's literacy abilities. Decide if you are going to give support by reading out each statement or leaving the child to do this alone.

Once the young person has decided which boxes to tick, look through the worksheet together, exploring the potential positive and negative consequences of each statement. Similarly, encourage empathy for other people's feelings – for example, how might parents or carers feel if their children don't come home on time or lie? How do they feel if someone lies to them? Close the session by thinking of three examples where it is vital to tell the truth.

THE TRUTH, THE WHOLE TRUTH...

Look at the statements below and consider how true they are for you. Please put a tick in the box that is most like you.

Statement	That's me.	That's sometimes me.	That's not me.
Sometimes I tell a lie to get out of trouble.			
I don't always tell my parent or carer where I have been.			
At school I say I am ill to get out of lessons.			
I know it is important to tell the truth.			
If a police officer asked me questions, I would tell the truth			

I sometimes lie about my age to get into the cinema.			
If a teacher asked about any of my friends, I wouldn't tell on them.			
I often tell people I have got things that I haven't.			
If my sister asks if I like her new clothes, I say 'yes' even if I don't.			
Sometimes I pretend I can't hear my mum when she tells me to do something.			
If I found £20 at school, I would pretend it was mine.			

2.8 This is me!

This is a fun way of encouraging young people to share things about themselves and to get an idea of what motivates them. It works just as well as a group or an individual activity.

Aim

The aim of the activity is to produce a collage plate that represents a young person's personality.

You will need

- large paper plates
- glue
- scissors
- marker pens
- magazines (age-appropriate)
- newspaper
- varnish.

How to do it

Divide the children into groups of four and hand out scissors, glue, magazines and paper plates. If you are doing this as part of a one-to-one session, share this process with the child, discussing the child's choices as you go along.

Explain to the group that the idea is for everyone to use the text and illustrations from the newspaper and magazines to produce a plate that represents their personality. This can include the good and bad bits! Offer a few ideas, for example headlines about their favourite pop stars, or pictures that show how they may be feeling today. If the young people look a bit unsure, you and your co-worker can have a go at making one too.

Encourage the children to 'own' their plates by signing their collages with decorative versions of their names. The glitter glue is really effective for this!

Once everyone has finished, suggest the young people display their plates, and invite them to ask questions of each other and share information.

Finally, when the glue has dried, varnish the plates to seal the pictures and use them to decorate the group area.

2.9 Attitude scale

This is a good way to start work around self-esteem and encourages young people to say what they want. It introduces the idea of assertive and passive behaviour.

Aim

To encourage young people to think about how they see themselves, and then consider how this compares with how others perceive them.

You will need

- nothing!

How to do it

Explain to the young people that the aim of this activity is to develop an attitude scale to show the personalities within the group ranging from 'assertive' to 'passive'. You may need to offer further explanation of what you mean by assertive and passive. The scale should form a straight line and include everyone.

Decide which end of your scale is 'assertive' and which end is 'passive' and make sure that the young people are clear about this.

Allow five to ten minutes (depending on the size of the group) for the young people to decide where they think they should stand on the scale. Position yourself on the scale too. When everybody is comfortable with their positions on the scale, stop.

Ask the young people to look around them and reflect on what they see. Are there any surprises? Does how they see themselves fit in with other people's perception of them?

2.10 Colours

This activity encourages children to discuss their feelings and emotions. It can be used either individually or with small groups.

Aim

To look at colours and the feelings associated with them.

You will need

- pens
- squares of card in assorted colours.

How to do it

Begin the session by introducing the idea that colours can represent feelings and emotions. Make sure you stress that this is not an exact science! Different colours may mean different things to different people. A good example of this is the colour red, which can mean anger, heat or passion to different people.

Hand out the coloured squares with a pen. One at a time, call out the colours, asking the young people to look carefully at the corresponding square and to think about the emotions they associate with it before writing these onto the square.

When everybody has finished, ask the whole group to form a circle and discuss what has been written on the squares. Does everyone have the same word? Are there any patterns or themes emerging? Go on to consider the impact that colour can have on the environment – for example, what colours would the group choose to decorate a room to relax in, have a party in, or even do homework in?

Finally, invite the children in turn to select a colour that they believe represents how they feel now.

2.11 Helping hand

This session can be done either as a group or a one-to-one activity. It is a good start to a project about keeping safe or protective behaviours.

Aim

To encourage children to identify people they could talk to if they were worried or concerned about an issue.

You will need

- paper
- pens.

How to do it

Before you start, consider the make-up of your group and how much you know about the young people in it. If you have not worked with the group before you will need to be very careful to keep the information discussed depersonalised by referring only to the examples below. If you know the group members well, you can ask them to think of their own situations. However, be careful that you do not encourage the young people to make disclosures unless you have the appropriate support in place.

Ask the group members to form a circle or to sit so that they can all hear you and contribute.

Choose one of the situations below and read it out to the young people.

John is ten, wears glasses and is the smallest in his class. He hates sports, but is really good at maths and always comes top in tests. The other kids all laugh, call him 'boffin' and 'goody-goody' and 'teacher's pet' and take his glasses out of his bag and throw them to each other in the cloakroom…

Cherish is nine and is friends with some older girls who live on the same estate. The older girls have started stealing things from the local shop. Cherish has not taken anything, but she has eaten some stolen sweets the girls gave her. Now the others in the group are saying that they won't let her hang around with them if she does not steal too…

Then ask the question, 'How do you think Tom/Cherish feels?', and facilitate a discussion around the answers given.

Next ask the children to imagine that they are in a similar situation. Explain that they do not have to share what they are thinking, but suggest that they start to identify people whom they could tell and ask for help.

Hand out the paper and pens and ask the young people to draw around one of their hands in the centre of their sheet.

Now explain that the thumb on the hand represents the first person that they would go to if they were in trouble and needed help. Ask them to write down whom they would go to next if the first person wasn't in or would not listen. Carry on until all five fingers have names.

Reflect on the process with the group. Was it easy to identify a support network? Will it change often? What is it about the people chosen that makes them special and different from others the children know?

2.12 Would you ever...?

This sheet is best used with small groups of children or young people whom you feel are at risk of becoming involved in offending behaviour. You will need to have a good relationship with them so that they feel they can be honest.

The young people's responses will define any follow-up sessions. These should highlight the choices that can be made and the consequences of getting involved with behaviour that is likely to lead to offending.

Aim

This session helps to identify offending behaviour and to assess the need for preventative work to address the issues and concerns of young people.

You will need

- some information about the law and how it relates to children over ten years old

- copies of the 'would you ever...?' sheet

- pens.

How to do it

When you first introduce this sheet you will need to reassure the young people that what they share will remain confidential, unless it is a child protection issue or you are required to pass it on to the police. You will have to assess the group members and their level of offending to see if this is going to be a major issue.

Also, make sure that the young people realise that you are not suggesting that you think they have done any or all of the behaviours on the list! If you know that the group members have a short attention span, cut the number of questions you ask. Similarly you could read the questions out.

Pick out any issues that you want the group to explore and facilitate a discussion. Provide information and ask if the young people would like to focus on one or two issues to work on over the next few weeks.

If you want to use this activity as part of your project evaluation, ask the questions once at the start of your involvement with the group and again towards the end to see if there are any changes in attitudes or behaviour. You will need to code the sheets so you know who said what!

WOULD YOU EVER...?

For every question please answer 'yes' or 'no'.

Would you ever...	Yes	No
text abuse to someone you don't like?		
call someone names in the street?		
give a false name to the police?		
steal something from a shop?		
steal money from your friends?		
steal money from home?		
steal things from home to sell?		
be unkind to an animal?		
throw stones at the window of a neighbour you didn't like?		
write things about another child on a wall?		
damage cars parked in the street?		
keep money you found in the street?		
hit someone who called you names?		
use someone else's mobile phone without asking?		
travel on a bus or train without paying?		

2.13 Feelings file

This encourages children to focus on a specific feeling and recall the events surrounding it. It is a good prelude to activities in the next section that look at how emotions are expressed.

Aim

For young people to begin to associate feelings with events and actions.

You will need

- to copy the headings below onto A4 paper (approx. 8½ × 11") to make 'feelings file' sheets

- pens.

How to do it

Ask the young people to choose a partner. If there is an uneven number in the group, work in threes.

Hand out a pen and a copy of the 'feelings file' sheet to each member of the group.

Explain that during this exercise individuals are free to choose how much they want to share, and that they have the right to withhold things they do not want to discuss. This gives them all the opportunity to choose only examples that they feel comfortable with.

Ask the young people to read the sheet on their own, looking at each heading and thinking about a time when they felt like this. For example, a time when they felt angry could be last night during an argument with their brother or sister over what to watch on television.

When they have all had time to think about the task and select words that reflect their experience, ask them to share their sheets with their partners. Spend time comparing and discussing what has been written. Are they similar? Expand on what situations these feelings might be associated with. Ask the young people to discuss how they handle different situations – for example, feeling lonely or excited.

Close the session by asking them all to choose a word to describe how they feel now.

Headings

A time that I felt happy was...

A time that I felt angry was...

A time that I felt excited was...

I last felt sad when...

The last time I was lonely was...

A time that I felt loved was...

A person who makes me laugh is...

A person who makes me feel loved is...

A person who I trust is...

Someone who does not help me is...

Someone who I can talk to about these things is...

2.14 Things about me

This is a good way to initiate conversation during a first session. You can use the worksheet with any age from nine years old, but it is not appropriate for a group activity.

Aim

To encourage children to focus on their positive skills and qualities, and to identify areas that they would like support with.

You will need

- coloured pens
- a copy of the 'things about me – signpost' sheet.

How to do it

Before you hand out the 'signpost' sheet, spend some time talking about the aim of the activity and what you would like the child to produce. Explain that the process enables you to understand a child's interests, wishes and needs, and that children can tell you as much or as little as they choose.

Give out the worksheet and allow the young person time and space to think about responses. If a child is struggling, make some suggestions to illustrate what you are asking. For example, something done well could be drawing or playing football; something to work on could be controlling anger.

Together, look at the completed 'signpost' and use the issues raised to develop an action plan to work on during subsequent sessions. You may want to consider using the template offered in activity 1.3, 'My action plan', or devising something similar that sets out clear, achievable goals to work towards. Give a copy to the young person so that you are both clear about the aims of your meetings.

THINGS ABOUT ME – SIGNPOST

Have a look at the 'signpost' below and use the spaces to write key words that describe you. Think of things you do well, what is special about you and things you like, and put these on the white signs. On the grey signs, put things you think are not going so well or that you would like help with.

Chapter 3

Expressing Yourself

3.1 Picture pairs

This is a 'matching' game that can be used with young people who have difficulties in reading and prefer to work with pictures. You can either facilitate the game between two players or play the game with a young person as part of an individual plan.

Aim

To encourage children to recognise non-verbal signals and expressions and so respond appropriately to situations.

You will need

- a set of cards with faces showing different expressions and emotions – two of each card.

How to do it

Before the session, prepare by making up the cards. You can be as creative as you like with the pictures, but remember to make a matching 'pair' for each one. These could be hand-drawn images of faces expressing different feelings – happy smiles or angry frowns. Another method is to cut faces out of magazines. Make sure that you have a good range of expressions.

Place the cards face down on the table and muddle them up so that the pairs are not together. Explain to the children that this is a game of memory and that they need to watch what is happening. Take it in turns to turn over two cards and look at the pictures. Encourage the child to tell you what the person on the card is feeling and discuss how this is recognised.

If the cards are the same, they form a 'pair' and can be collected. If not, once you have identified the face, place it face down back in the same position. The person to make up the most pairs wins.

3.2 Act out feelings!

This activity can be used as a 'taster' for more in-depth drama or role-play sessions to address specific issues. It should be played at a fairly fast pace so that everybody has the chance to 'act out' a character.

Aim

To enable group members to 'act out' issues in a safe environment.

You will need

- to make a set of 'act out' cards with different feelings written on them

- information around issues likely to be raised through the session – for example, bullying.

How to do it

Before the session make a set of 'act out' cards by writing different feelings onto small pieces of card or paper. Ideas include 'Fear', 'Happiness', 'Sadness', 'Pride', 'Disappointment', 'Loneliness', 'Anxiety', 'Frustration', 'Confidence', 'Boredom' and 'Anger'.

Start the session with a short discussion about how non-verbal communication shows others how we are feeling or behaving without any words being spoken. Ask the young people to consider how true this is and to think about their own body language.

Next, explain that you are going to ask for a volunteer to demonstrate this. Introduce the set of cards and tell the group that while one person is 'acting out' the feeling written on the card, the others should ask questions to try to guess what is on the card. All questions must be answered in character; for example, if your card says 'Anger', you can reply to the question 'How are you?' by shouting, 'What has it got to do with you?'

If you are met with a shy silence, volunteer yourself or your co-worker to take the first turn. Often this is a great success, especially if you really over-act!

A guess can be made at any stage in the process. If it is correct, the person who guessed takes a new card and begins again. If the guess is wrong, continue until someone gets it right. Try to keep the questions moving along so that the game keeps pace.

This should be a game that is thought provoking but good fun. Be aware that some cards may be uncomfortable for the young person who draws it to 'act out'. For example, a young person who has been the victim of a bully may not be happy to 'act out' being scared or even being a bully. You will need to be sensitive and, if necessary, be prepared to swap cards.

3.3 Talk, talk

This discussion is aimed at young people who have poor social skills and find it hard to make friends or express themselves clearly. The idea can be adapted to suit either a group or an individual setting and works well with activity 3.4, 'Reflective listening'.

Aim

This session considers the difference between talking 'to' and talking 'with' someone, and promotes conversation to develop verbal communication skills.

You will need

- marker pens
- two large sheets of flipchart paper.

How to do it

Before the young people arrive, stick up the two sheets of paper so that the whole group can see them. Write the heading 'Talking' on the top of one sheet and 'Conversation' on the other.

Explain the aim of the session and ask for two volunteers. Make sure you facilitate this part carefully, bearing in mind the literacy skills within the group.

Ask the group to consider what they think the differences are between 'talking' and having a 'conversation'.

Hand each volunteer a marker pen to write down suggestions from the group. If the response is slow to begin with, make some suggestions. For example:

Talking:

Saying things

Telling about things that are important to you

Conversation:

Talking and listening

Sharing information

Once the young people have exhausted their ideas, facilitate a discussion around the points raised.

3.4 Reflective listening

This introduces the concept of reflective listening to a group. It develops conversational skills and encourages interest in what others say. You can use the activity with any size group because the young people are asked to work in threes or fours.

Aim

To focus group members on a discussion that will enable them to get to know each other quickly. If the children are already friends, then it should highlight things that they don't know about each other. It encourages the young people to listen carefully to what is being said and to think about it, rather than cutting in with their own opinions.

You will need

- nothing!

How to do it

Depending on the numbers of children you have in the group, ask them to work in threes or fours. If it is a really small group, it does work in pairs. Discuss confidentiality at this stage and reach an agreement that what is shared in the group stays there. This should encourage the participants to feel safe about talking personally.

Specify a topic to discuss within the group: 'What people usually think about me when they first meet me is...' You can demonstrate this by giving an example to start them off: 'What people think about me when they first meet me is that I have a good sense of humour!'

Set a ground rule that only one member can talk at a time in the group and that the others should listen and think about what is being said.

Once all the children have had their say, discuss the information given within the groups. In particular, invite them to share first impressions and then consider how these have changed as they have got to know each other.

3.5 Don't laugh at me!

This worksheet can be used in a group setting, but it works best one to one where young people have more time to think through the issues raised.

Aim

To reflect on how it feels to be laughed at, and to build empathy for other children who may be in that situation. It also encourages children to consider strategies for coping with bullying and to identify who could offer them support.

You will need

- to prepare a 'Don't laugh at me!' sheet for each child using flipchart paper
- pens.

How to do it

Prepare flipchart sheets by writing the headings below, leaving space in between for the child to write their responses:

The last time someone laughed at me was...

How it felt...

What I did...

What I could do differently...

What I will do next time...

Introduce the idea that, as well as an expression of joy and amusement, laughter can also be used to make people feel uncomfortable or stupid. Explain that this is the difference between laughing 'at' someone and 'with' them.

Hand out the worksheets and ask the children how they feel if someone laughs 'with' them, reinforcing the positive feelings that shared laughter generates. Then move on to consider the last time someone laughed 'at' them – for example friends, a parent or siblings. Encourage them to share the experience and write down on their sheet how it made them feel.

Discuss what the young people could do if this happened again – for example, walk away and tell a trusted adult or friend. Review together what they have written. Is this a solution that is going to resolve the issue or cause more trouble? Spend time doing this and then ask the young people which strategy they think is most likely to work for them. These can then be recorded as goals for next time.

Finally, agree 'safe' people to ask for support from if this should happen in the future.

3.6 Images

This activity works on the assumption that how we see ourselves and how we are seen are not always the same.

Aim

The idea of the activity is to start young people exploring the idea that how they perceive themselves is not necessarily how others view them. It encourages discussion around public image and first impression, and questions the importance of these.

You will need

- a list of personal attributes written up and displayed
- two sheets of paper for each person
- pens.

How to do it

In advance, write up the following list of attributes onto a large sheet of paper and display it where all the young people will be able to see it. Read it out before you start the activity to make sure everyone knows what is on it.

Good sense of humour	Confident
Good listener	Honest
Supports friends who need it	Good at understanding
Shy	Quiet

Does not blame others	Trustworthy
Withdrawn	Aggressive
Bad tempered	Dishonest
Fun to be with	Boastful
Creative and full of ideas	Popular
Moody	Sad
Loud	Good at explaining
Trouble maker	Rude

Explain the aim of the session to the group and ask the young people to choose a partner to work with. Hand each person two sheets of paper and a pen.

Now ask the young people to turn away from their partners and have a look at the list of attributes displayed. Working with their backs to their partners, ask each person to complete both sheets:

Sheet 1: Write down the words that you think describe your partner.

Sheet 2: Write down the words that you think describe yourself.

Allow up to 15 minutes for everybody to complete the task, and then ask the young people to turn around and face their partners. Then, in turn, ask everyone to feed back what they have written and compare this with how their partners see themselves. Are these the same? Are characteristics seen in different ways? For example, a young person may have ticked 'shy' as a personal attribute, but their partner may see this as 'sad'. Encourage the young people to focus on positive attributes and discuss areas of difference.

3.7 Late for school!

This provides the opportunity for young people to re-write a typical scenario the way they think it should be. Depending on how big your group is, you can do a storyboard for as many characters as you like that shows the different perspectives when a young person is late for school – again! If you are working individually ask the young person to create just one storyline that shows all the characters.

Aim

To encourage young people to think of the consequences of oversleeping and getting to school late, and the impact that this has on different family members as well as themselves.

You will need

- a sheet of flipchart paper for each group
- marker pens.

How to do it

Read out the following scenario to the whole group:

You stayed up late last night to watch your favourite TV programme. Your mum is calling you to get up but all you want to do is turn over and go back to sleep. You know this is the second time this week you have been late for school and your teacher has already noticed.

Despite her yells, you crawl back under the duvet wondering why your mum has to make such a fuss about everything. It's only maths first lesson and everyone knows you are no good at that. Perhaps you could go in later?

In groups of three or four using a flipchart sheet and marker pens, ask the young people to construct a comic strip to show what happens next.

Give each group the task of telling the story from a different character's point of view. The characters are:

- the young person
- the mum or dad
- the teacher.

Invite each group to present their storyboard, encouraging questions after each round to explore the potential consequences of any actions taken. Ask for different ideas to resolve the situation positively, and identify those actions that are likely to make the situation worse.

3.8 That makes me angry!

This works best when done individually.

Aim

This exercise encourages children and young people to begin to identify anger 'triggers' and so develop anger management techniques.

You will need

- copies of the 'that makes me angry!' sheet
- paper and pens.

How to do it

Begin the session by talking about anger as a valid emotion that everyone feels at some time. Ask the children to try to remember the last time they were angry, what happened and what their response to the situation was.

Hand out the 'that makes me angry!' sheets. Read out each point in turn, asking the young people to number it and then place two ticks next to the number if the example situation is likely to make them *very* angry, one tick if it would make them *a little* angry, a question mark if it may or may not make them angry, and a cross if it would not make them angry at all. They should decide based on the response that is most likely if the example situation happened to them.

Once everyone has finished, facilitate a whole group feedback session. Encourage the young people to explain why something – for example being laughed at – makes them very angry, and another thing doesn't.

The young people can then begin to identify 'triggers' for their own anger and to realise that we all have different anger thresholds or tolerances. From this you can begin work on strategies to cope with anger and aggression.

THAT MAKES ME ANGRY!

Someone calls you names in front of your friends.

You get laughed at for coming last in games.

You get blamed for something you didn't do.

Your bedtime is earlier than your friends'.

A teacher tells you to get out of class.

Your dad calls you 'thick' in front of your friends.

Someone steals your money at school.

A group of people you don't know start shouting abuse.

Your sister rightly accuses you of stealing her money.

Someone spreads untrue rumours about you.

Your mum grounds you for being rude.

Someone tells on you and you get in trouble.

Your mum won't give you any money.

Your team loses at football.

Your bike is stolen.

No one will listen to what you are trying to say.

3.9 I don't want to!

This encourages young people to develop strategies to say 'no' effectively in difficult situations. I have used it with both small groups and individually. You can vary the exercise by changing the issue featured in the scenario.

Aim

To develop assertiveness in saying 'no' to peer pressure to do things young people are uncomfortable with.

You will need

- a sheet of flipchart paper for each group
- pens.

How to do it

Read out the scenario below to the children.

You are walking to school with two of your friends. They tell you that they are going to miss school today and go into town, and ask you to go too. You know you should go to school but don't want to look silly in front of your friends. They turn round and set off for town, calling to you to hurry up. You know you will get into trouble if you get caught, but you don't want to let your friends down – what can you do?

Divide the young people into two groups and hand out a sheet of flipchart paper and pens to each. Group 1 should storyboard what could happen if the young person gives in to peer pressure and goes into town. Group 2 should storyboard the potential consequences if the character in the scenario doesn't join in with the friends and goes to school.

Ask both groups to come together and share storyboards. Use this as a basis for a discussion on peer pressure related back to the given scenario.

Encourage the young people to think about the consequences of the characters' actions. How could they say what they think assertively? How easy is it to say 'no' to friends? What could be done to resolve any potential conflict between the young people in the story?

3.10 My home

Before you start this activity make sure that you are aware of a group's living arrangements. For example, children who have recently moved, are living with foster parents, or have recently been bereaved may find it very difficult to discuss how they feel. This does not preclude using this process, but it may be too sensitive to do as a group.

Aim

To support children and young people in expressing how they feel about 'home' and their roles and responsibilities within it.

You will need

- nothing!

How to do it

Start the session by explaining that you would like the group to think about a statement that you are going to make. Explain that you would like those people who agree with it to raise their hands. Those who don't agree should keep hands down.

A home is just a place you sleep.

Once the young people have voted, invite them to share their opinions. So, for example, Kara could say she agrees because 'It is the people not the place that make a home', but Jake may think it is wrong because 'A home is somewhere you belong and are safe.'

Facilitate a discussion that asks the children for suggestions of what they can do to contribute towards making their home the way they want it. This can be emotional support, as well as practical things like household chores.

Finally, agree one thing each that they can do to make a positive difference for the next week. This could be something practical like picking up their dirty laundry or something such as not fighting with siblings. Review next time the group meets.

3.11 Name that feeling!

This can either be facilitated as a one-to-one discussion, or as a group activity as shown below.

Aim

This activity encourages children and young people to identify how they feel in different circumstances and encourages them to consider solutions that will not lead to tension and aggression.

You will need

- a large sheet of paper with the headings from the 'name that feeling' list written on it, folded into a concertina (accordion style) so that only the first scenario shows.

How to do it

Begin the session by talking about the wide range of emotions that we all feel. Introduce the idea that sometimes these feelings either get in the way of how we deal with a situation or are not identified correctly. So the problem remains unresolved, or becomes larger and we feel less able to deal with it. Ask the children to think about a time when a problem got worse because of something they did or did not do. What feelings do they remember?

Hand out the 'name that feeling' sheet, folded up so that only the first scenario can be seen. Sit in a circle and hand the sheet to the first young person with the request to read the situation aloud and consider the questions posed at the top of the sheet. If you know this will be a difficult task for your group, read each scenario out to the children.

After the first child has responded, facilitate a group feedback to get other people's opinions, before passing the paper on and unfolding the next scenario. Does everyone agree about the feelings that might arise? How easy is it to find solutions? Finally encourage the group to think about some examples of their own to share and work through together.

NAME THAT FEELING!

For each of the situations below think about the following:

- What is the problem?

- What is the feeling?

- What can be done?

1. Your friend always has more pocket money than you. It is not fair! Your mum is so mean. She says to do jobs around the house if you want more cash!

2. Your dad has left home to live with his new girlfriend. He said you could stay at weekends but now his girlfriend is saying that there is not enough room.

3. Someone at school is calling your brother names and threatening to break his electric wheelchair.

4. Your friend won an art competition at school. You are really fed up and think it must have been a fix. You know yours was better!

5. Your accent is different from the rest of your class. One girl keeps mimicking your voice and teasing you to make everyone laugh.

6. The class is kept in after school for something you did. Now everyone is telling you to own up or else…

3.12 Feeling valued

It is important for young people's self-esteem for them to feel valued by the people they care about. It is also important for them to build skills so that they value themselves too. Feeling undervalued and having low self-esteem can lead to frustration and aggressive behaviour as young people strive to get attention.

Aim

This worksheet is devised as an introduction to building self-worth.

You will need

- copies of the 'feeling valued' worksheet.

How to do it

Start by introducing the idea of self-esteem and feeling good about yourself. Hand out the worksheet and some pens. If you know that a young person finds reading and writing difficult, read the sheet out and use pictures or write down their answers yourself.

Support the children as they think about the issues raised on the sheet. If they say they cannot think of anything to write, suggest they think about the last time that someone made them feel happy or loved. You can then ask prompt questions to try to expand and reflect on this.

Once they have completed the sheet, review what has been written, in particular reflecting on what they have written in the final section. For example, young people may write that they feel valued when 'their mum praises them', and a way to achieve this could be 'to walk away when my brother starts a fight rather than hitting him which upsets my mum'. Devise an action plan with each young person to achieve some of these goals.

Review agreements made regularly to celebrate achievements and set new goals.

FEELING VALUED

This is me . . . .
. . . .
. . . .
. . . .
. . . .
. . . .
. . . .
. . . .
. . . .

Last time I felt valued was
when . . . .
. . . .
. . . .
. . . .
. . . .
. . . .
It made me feel . . . .
. . . .

People who make me feel good about myself are . . . .

. . . .

because . . . .

. . . .

I show them I am happy by . . . .

. . . .

Things that make me feel good about myself are:

1.

2.

3.

Things that I can do to help achieve this are:

1.

2.

3.

Chapter 4

Making Friends

4.1 Friendship line

This is a good way to look at friendships past and present and the importance of them to our personal 'history'.

Aim

This activity enables young people to create friendship lines, which chart important people and their influences on their lives.

You will need

- sheets of flipchart paper
- marker pens.

How to do it

Hand each member of the group a sheet of flipchart paper and place a good selection of markers close by.

Explain to the young people that they are each going to make a 'friendship line' to depict people whose friendship has been important to them from their earliest memories to the present. This can be done using words or pictures.

Next to each name, ask the group members to show why that person was or is important to them.

While explaining the task, stress that it is up to each person to choose how much they wish to put down onto paper and share. Also point out that it does not matter how many or how few people are recorded on the line – this is an exercise to look at friendships and what they mean, not a competition to see who knows the most people!

Once everyone has finished, ask the group members to come together and talk through the parts of their friendship line that they feel comfortable sharing. Are there similarities? Have people kept in touch with their early friends? Are some friendships associated with different activities – for example, Scouts or Irish dancing?

4.2 What makes a good friend?

This worksheet works well at the start of a session because it encourages young people to be open about their first thoughts before any discussions take place.

Aim

The aim of the activity is to identify the key features of a good friend and to encourage children to consider what they can offer a potential relationship.

You will need

- pens
- A4 sheets (approx. 8½ × 11") of coloured paper.

How to do it

If you are planning this as part of a group session, gather the children together into a circle. If you are working individually, you could write the points onto a large sheet of flipchart paper and encourage the young people to illustrate the things that they record.

Explain to the group that the idea of the activity is to start to think about what goes into making a good friendship. Encourage the children to consider friendship as a two-way process that needs working at if it is to be successful. This means that they have a responsibility to make it work as well as the other person!

Hand out the paper and ask the children to write the following under the heading, 'What makes a good friend?'

Three things that I think make a good friend are:

1.

2.

3.

What makes me a good friend is:

1.

2.

3.

. . . . is my friend because

. . . .

I am a good friend to them because . . . .

. . . .

Good things we do together are:

1.

2.

3.

Allow about 15 minutes for the children to fill in the gaps with their own ideas and thoughts. Ask that they work alone at the moment and stress that there are no definite right or wrong answers.

Once everyone has finished, divide the group into pairs and invite them to share sheets. Bring the children back together into a circle to discuss their ideas. Are there similar suggestions? Are some suggestions based on physical attributes or status within the group? For example, 'looking really good' or 'knowing everyone in town' may be seen as good qualities, but are they really the basis for a friendship?

Pull out the main themes and agree a group list. Display to refer to in future sessions about friends and relationships.

4.3 Magic spell for a friend

This is similar to the previous activity, but works well with children under 11 years old. It encourages them to think about what qualities they look for in a friend, what makes a person special and how to value friendship. It can be used with groups or individually.

Aim

To identify the key features that make a trusting friendship.

You will need

- a copy of the 'magic spell for a friend' worksheet for each child

- pens.

How to do it

Copy enough sheets for each group member to have one, and hand out with a pen. Ask everyone to imagine that you hold a 'magic wand' that will grant each person their 'ideal friend' if they can write the correct spell. This spell can summon up a real or imagined person who has the personal qualities that they think are vital for a good friendship. These personal qualities are not about how someone looks or what material things they have.

When the children have had time to think, ask them to list six things for the 'spell' that they think are the most important. After each attribute, there is a space on the worksheet to write a reason why this is a positive attribute and offer an example. If you know that some members of your group are not confident with writing tasks, divide the group into pairs so that a less confident child can work with another with good literacy skills.

Once everyone has finished, facilitate a group discussion that considers the following questions:

- Do people all want the same thing in a friendship?

- Are the things listed realistic to want in a friend?

- Are the characteristics that they value in others similar to things they themselves offer a friend?

MAGIC SPELL FOR A FRIEND

Write a spell to conjure up a friend who will be special to you.

1. . . . .

   This is important to me because . . . .

   . . . .

   . . . .

2. . . . .

   This is important to me because . . . .

   . . . .

   . . . .

3. . . . .

   This is important to me because . . . .

   . . . .

   . . . .

4. . . . .

   This is important to me because . . . .

   . . . .

   . . . .

5. . . . .

   This is important to me because . . . .

   . . . .

   . . . .

6. . . . .

   This is important to me because . . . .

   . . . .

   . . . .

4.4 Follow the crowd

You can alter the situations in this activity to fit issues relevant to the children you are working with.

Aim

This exercise asks young people to consider the consequences of their actions in potential situations and to consider the losses and gains of giving in to peer pressure.

You will need

- paper
- pens.

How to do it

Ask the young people to remember a time when they have 'followed the crowd' and done something that they knew was not right because friends were doing it. Explain that they do not have to share this unless they really want to, but encourage them to think about the choices they had and what made the decision for them.

Hand out paper and pens and explain that you are going to read out a selection of scenarios. After each one the children should write down what they think the 'plus' and 'minus' points for following the crowd would be. Encourage them to think ahead about the consequences of their decisions. For example, if a group of friends write their names on a wall and you decide to join in, the 'plus' might be that you become accepted as part of the group. The 'minus' point might be that a neighbour sees it, recognises you and tells your parents.

When all the scenarios have been worked through, invite feedback, discussing potential 'plus' and 'minus' points for each.

Conclude by facilitating a discussion that looks at ways that the young person in the situations could have been assertive and said 'no' without losing face within the peer group.

Scenarios

1. Joining in with a group of young people who are bullying another child at school.

2. Joining in with a group who are being unkind to a stray cat.

3. Joining in with a group who are cheating in a game against younger children.

4. Joining in with friends who are lying to their parents to get out of trouble.

5. Joining in with a group who are staying out in the street later than they are allowed.

6. Joining in with a friend who is taking other children's things without asking.

7. Joining in with a group who are being rude to a teacher.

4.5 Jealousy bag

This is thought provoking but good fun! You will need to be sensitive to potential emotions that the activity may bring to the surface, and allow time for discussion.

Aim

This activity enables children to identify and share things that arouse jealousy, and it also provokes discussion.

You will need

- sticky notes
- pens
- an opaque bag.

How to do it

Ask the group members to make a large circle and sit down. Pass around sticky notes and a pen to each young person. Ask them to write on each piece of paper one thing that makes them feel jealous. Make sure you explain that the slips will be shared later, although they will remain anonymous.

If the young people seem slow to start, make a few suggestions. This could be something like 'my friend having more money than me' or 'my friend being better at football than I am'.

Once the slips of paper have been written on, they should be folded so no one else can see what has been written. Then place them in the bag. Collect the bag and shake it so that the papers get mixed up well. Now pass the bag back around the circle in the opposite direction.

The young people take the bag in turn, pull out a slip and read the contents. If they pick out their own, they should fold it back up and return it for someone else to pick out and read. Leave space for comments or a short discussion after each reading. Are there any duplications or similar themes? Does everyone feel jealous at some stage? Discuss strategies to cope with this emotion.

4.6 Get knotted!

This team game is really good fun for groups of eight or more. It is a good way to start a session about team work because a joint effort is required if it is to be successful.

Aim

This activity encourages young people to start to work together to achieve a group goal.

You will need

- nothing!

How to do it

Ask the group members to make a circle, standing next to each other but not so close that they are touching. Then tell them to join hands with two other members of the circle, but not with anyone standing next to them. This is a lot harder than it seems!

Allow about ten minutes for everyone to be included, making sure that no one is cheating and everyone is holding onto two other people.

When everybody is in place, ask the young people to stop, hold their poses and look about them to see what shape the group has formed.

Then set the young people the task of untying themselves and re-forming the circle – without breaking hands!

You should end up with the whole group back in a circle, though not necessarily all facing the same way!

4.7 My space

You need an even number of participants for this activity.

Aim

This is a really good way of introducing the concept of 'personal space' and illustrating that we all have different boundaries and comfort zones.

You will need

- chalk or a strip of coloured tape.

How to do it

Divide the group into two equal smaller groups. Draw a chalk line half-way across the room. If you have coloured tape, stick a strip across the floor in the middle of the room. Try to ensure that there are no trip hazards.

Ask Group 1 to stand along the wall in a row facing into the room.

Group 2 should now form a straight line along the chalk mark or coloured strip, opposite Group 1.

Ask Group 1 to move slowly towards Group 2, from the opposite side of the area, with their arms outstretched. Group 2 should stand as still as possible.

Members of Group 2 should raise their hands in front of their chests as soon as a young person from Group 1 comes uncomfortably close to them.

Once everyone has done this and all of Group 1 have a partner from Group 2, stop. Ask everyone to stay where they are and look about. The distance, or 'personal space', left between each couple will vary depending on what individuals feel comfortable with. Repeat the exercise with Group 2 walking towards Group 1, again looking at the space left.

Reflect and discuss with the group. This can then lead on to work around keeping safe and protective behaviour.

4.8 The bus stop

This is a drama-based activity designed to encourage young people to engage in role-play. It works best with smaller groups of young people who know each other enough to be confident in arguing their case!

Aim

To enable young people to practise formulating arguments and asserting themselves within a role-play environment.

You will need

- nothing!

How to do it

Explain to the young people that this activity revolves around a group of strangers waiting to catch a bus. Ask the group to nominate one person to be the 'bus driver'. This should not be you, the youth worker, because your role will be to facilitate what happens within the group.

The rest of the group stands in a line, representing a bus queue. Suggest that they formulate a character for themselves that explains why they are in the bus queue. If they are looking doubtful, offer a few ideas yourself – for example, a mother carrying shopping, a man coming home from work, a student coming back from college.

The bus driver pulls up and says to the queue, 'One place, and one place only'. Everyone in the queue then needs to present the reason why they should have the last place on the bus. Encourage the young people to be creative about the reasons they use to tell the bus driver why they need the place.

Remind them throughout the process that the final choice lies with the bus driver and only the driver says who gets the seat. Once the decision has been made, talk the experience through with the group. Did the young people think it was a good decision? What else could they have said to alter the bus driver's mind? How did it feel to have one person making the decision?

4.9 Picture squares

This activity illustrates the concept that a successful team is made up of individuals. If it is to work effectively, all members of the team need to work together to form a 'whole'.

Aim

The aim of this exercise is to work together to complete a picture. Everyone needs to do their part or the picture will remain incomplete and the task unfinished.

You will need

- a large picture
- art paper or card the same size as the picture
- mounting card or stiff paper the same size as the picture
- paint
- brushes
- water jars, etc.

How to do it

To prepare for the session, find a copy of a picture that you think will interest the group. This could be a famous painting, such as Van Gogh's *Sunflowers*, or a photo of a film star or singer. Try to find a picture that is fairly large so that the children can see the detail.

If you know that your group does not enjoy art or will struggle with copying a complex picture, consider choosing a well-known cartoon character.

Cut the picture into squares. You will need enough squares for the young people to have one each to study. Put the picture back together and display it on a table so that the children can see what they are aiming for.

Cut the art paper or card into squares of similar number and size.

Mark the squares on the mounting card or stiff paper.

When the group members arrive, show them the picture and ask them to look closely at it. Then take it apart and hand a piece to each child.

Show the young people the squares of art paper or card and explain the task. If you know that they will struggle, suggest they put the 'puzzle' back together onto the mounting board and pencil their names onto the squares that they are going to work on. This will stop frustration later.

Allow the group members enough time to work on their squares using the paint and brushes to copy the detail from the original picture square. The time allowed will depend on how skilled they are at drawing and/or how much they enjoy art activities.

Encourage the children to sign their square by painting their name around the edge of the picture. If this will look silly, you can ask them to sign around the edge of the finished picture once it is mounted.

Finally, when everything is dry and completed, put the squares together to form the picture on the mounting board. Put it on the wall with the original below it and review it with the group.

A variation of this would be to use a photo of each member of the group to make up the squares. Hand out the photos so that everyone is doing someone else and mount them at the end as a group picture of all the children.

Chapter 5

Endings

5.1 Positive thoughts

Aim

This evaluation encourages young people to think about the roles that other group members have played in making the session a success for them.

You will need

- nothing!

How to do it

Ask the group members to sit down in a wide circle. Explain that what you would like them to do is to say 'goodbye' and one positive thing to the person on their left and right in the circle.

Stress that only positive comments are welcome and make sure no one is left out or feels isolated. Include yourself and your co-worker in the process.

So for example, 'Goodbye Donna, I thought you worked really hard in our team game' or 'Goodbye Bradley, thanks for listening to me'.

Finally, go around the circle again and ask the children to say one positive thing about the group itself.

5.2 Today I...

A quick and easy evaluation method that needs no preparation. It works with any age and size of group.

Aim

To encourage young people to focus on one positive experience they have had during a session.

You will need

- nothing!

How to do it

Ask the young people to form a circle facing each other.

In turn, ask them to say, 'Today I...' followed by something positive that has happened to them during the session they have just taken part in. This can be factual, such as 'Today I met Neelam for the first time', or a response that focuses on feelings, such as 'Today I felt confident about standing up for myself'.

If someone is struggling to think of what to say, offer the option to 'pass' and return to that person at the end. Make sure no one feels uncomfortable or pressured into saying something complicated or talking about feelings that have arisen that they don't want to share with the group.

Close the group by offering a 'Today I...' of your own.

5.3 Faces

This is a very quick form of evaluation that needs little preparation and is suitable for children of all abilities.

Aim

To get instant feedback of how a session was received by young people in a very simple way.

You will need

- Post-it note for each group member
- good range of pens.

How to do it

Before the session, stick a large piece of coloured paper onto the wall. This will become your evaluation board at the end of the activity.

After you have finished the session, hand out a Post-it note and pen to each young person.

Ask the young people to think about how they feel having participated in the session, and then to draw a face to represent this on the Post-it note. This should be really simple and show either a smiley, straight or turned-down mouth to represent how they feel.

When they have drawn their 'face', ask them to stick the note onto the piece of coloured paper on the wall. Ask them to look at all the stickers. Are there mainly happy or sad faces?

Collect the stickers and use them as part of your evaluation for the session.

5.4 Circle time

Circles are good ways to end sessions so that everyone can see each other and nobody feels outside the group.

Aim

This activity gets feedback from each member of a group without interruption from the others.

You will need

- any small object that can be passed around the group.

How to do it

Ask the group members to form a circle with the youth workers.

Show the children the object that you have chosen. This could be something like a pen, but you could choose something with more significance. I have used a small teddy or a ball.

Explain that people can only speak when they are holding the object. When they have finished, they pass it onto the next member of the group.

Ask questions that will evaluate the session – for example, 'What part of this activity did you enjoy most?' and 'Name me one thing you learnt.' Make sure you ask the same question of each person to get an overall picture. The number of questions you ask will depend on the size of the group.

After the session, review the answers with your co-worker and record the findings.

5.5 Picture this...

This uses a drama technique for evaluating how young people feel about the experiences they have just shared. It is suitable for groups of all ages and ability.

Aim

To use a visualisation process to enable young people to assess their own feelings and learning.

You will need

- candles and matches (optional)
- music (optional).

How to do it

How you create a relaxed, calm environment is up to you and the area you have to work in. One suggestion is to light candles, dim the lights and play music quietly in the background. I have used New Age tapes of the sea and sea creatures to provide a tranquil setting to encourage the young people to relax.

Once you have 'set the scene', ask the children to either sit or lie down quietly with their eyes closed. You can use some basic relaxation techniques to focus the group, such as flexing and relaxing limbs, and breathing deeply.

As the group members begin to 'chill out', ask that they picture in their heads a swimming pool on a warm, sunny day. Describe the pool in detail, including a deep end with a diving board and a shallow end with steps out. You can be as creative as you want.

Now, suggest that everyone uses the image of the swimming pool in their head to represent the session they have just taken part in. Where do they see themselves? Struggling in the deep end or somewhere in the middle? Watching from the side or desperate to dive in? If visualisation is a new experience for the young people, use some of these suggestions to get them thinking of their own. Encourage the sharing of ideas. Finally, close the session by telling the group members to relax and open their eyes gradually as you count to 20.

5.6 Headlines

This is a group evaluation that produces a joint piece of work that depicts the collective experience. Because it takes time, you may want to use it during the final session of a project. You can use it with groups of up to six young people.

Aim

To produce a newspaper front page that shows the group experience of the project the young people have just taken part in.

You will need

- newspapers and magazines
- scissors
- glue
- large sheets of paper
- marker pens.

How to do it

Hand out paper, glue, scissors and markers to each group of four to six young people. Make available a good selection of magazines and newspapers. Explain to the children that the task is to create a newspaper front page to show what has been learnt or experienced during the project they have been working on.

Suggest that the young people use both marker pens and cut-out letters from the newspapers to make the 'headlines' and then devise their copy to go with it. This should include how they feel, what they liked best and anything the group members would like followed up in a further session.

Once the front pages are complete, display them on the wall and invite each group to review each other's, asking questions or explaining sections as they go along. Where possible, leave the headline pictures on display for other young people to see, potentially sparking interest and further discussion.

5.7 Gifts

This evaluation method takes longer to facilitate than some of the other methods given, so it is best used with small groups of children.

Aim

To encourage young people to recognise skills and qualities in each other and offer positive feedback at the end of the session. This increases confidence and helps build self-esteem.

You will need

- small pieces of paper
- pens
- opaque bag.

How to do it

Hand out pens and pieces of paper to each group member. Each person should have a piece of paper to represent each group member.

Explain that you would like them to write an individual message on their paper for each person in the group. This should be positive and relate to the session they have just taken part in, for example 'Ruben – thanks for making me laugh' or 'Siobhan – you always listen to everyone's ideas'.

Ask the children to fold their message unsigned, and to write the name of the person they intend to receive the 'gift' on the front.

Collect the 'gifts' and place them in the bag. Give it a good shake and then walk amongst the group distributing the slips of paper. Depending on the young people, they can either look at their 'gifts' within the group or take them away with them to read later.

All members of the group should now have some positive feedback about their contributions to the group process.